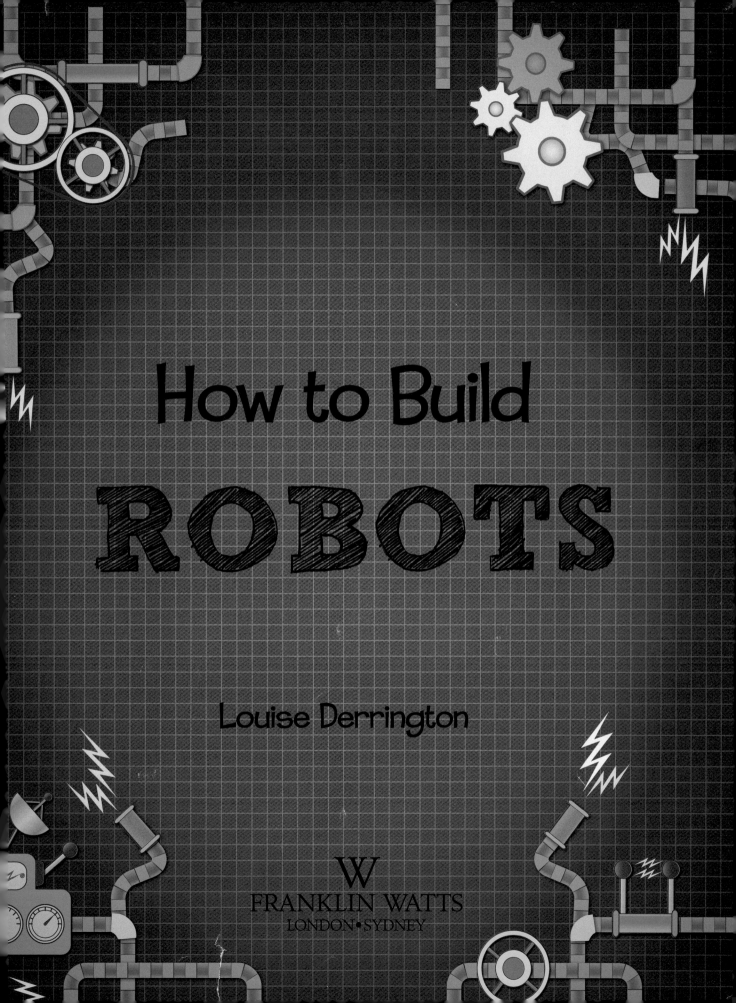

How to Build
ROBOTS

Louise Derrington

W
FRANKLIN WATTS
LONDON•SYDNEY

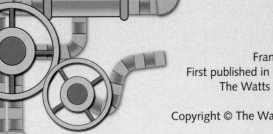

Franklin Watts
First published in Great Britain in 2016 by
The Watts Publishing Group

Credits
Executive editor: Adrian Cole
Packaged by: Storeybooks
Design manager: Peter Scoulding
Cover design and illustrations: Cathryn Gilbert

Dewey number 629.8'92
ISBN 978 1 4451 4467 2

Printed in China

MIX
Paper from
responsible sources
FSC® C104740

FSC
www.fsc.org

Photo credits:
The publishers would like to thank the following for permission to reproduce their
photos: Deymos.HR / Shutterstock.com: 15; D J Shin: 29 (top); Greg Mitchell – United
States Navy: 4 (bottom); Guzugi at English Wikipedia: 29 (bottom); Jon Ray: 5 (top);
NASA: 5 (middle); Xavier Caré / Wikimedia Commons / CC-BY-SA: 5: (bottom); Zen
wave: 4 (top).

Step-by-step photography by Tudor Photography, Banbury.

Every attempt has been made to clear copyright. Should there be any inadvertent
omission please apply to the publisher for rectification.

Franklin Watts
An imprint of
Hachette Children's Group
Part of The Watts Publishing Group
Carmelite House
50 Victoria Embankment
London EC4Y 0DZ

An Hachette UK Company
www.hachette.co.uk

www.franklinwatts.co.uk

CONTENTS

SAFETY FIRST

Some of the projects in this book require scissors, sharp tools or a hot glue gun. When using these things we would recommend that children are supervised by a responsible adult.

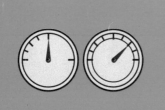

What is a robot?

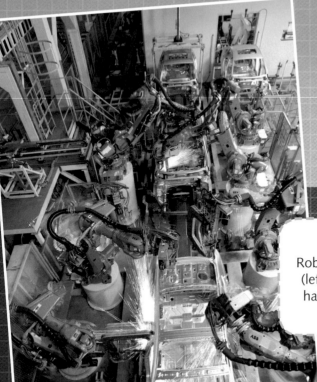

Robots are machines that are capable of carrying out a series of actions automatically. They perform complicated, useful and sometimes dangerous jobs. They are intelligent machines but, unlike humans, they cannot think for themselves.

Robots in the workplace

Robots have changed the way we make things, from cars (left) to computers. Robots do not get bored when they have to do the same things over and over again, which makes them very efficient.

Robots in danger

Robots help us in some of the most dangerous places on Earth. They are used to detect and dispose of bombs. They can also be fitted with sensors and be sent into contaminated areas to collect information about levels of chemicals and radiation.

Robots in medicine

Robots are already used by doctors performing surgery. Researchers are investigating many more ways that robots could be useful, including the development of tiny robots which will be able to squeeze through the narrowest blood vessels to perform medical procedures.

The new generation of prostheses (artificial limbs) are called myoelectrics. These robotic limbs are powered by electrical signals from the remaining muscles of the limb (right).

Robots in the home

As more and more people study robotics, they come up with inventive ideas for how robots can help us at home. Indoors, there are robot cleaners to wash floors and vacuum carpets. Outdoors, there are robots to mow the lawn and clean swimming pools. In Japan and elsewhere, research is underway to see whether robot pets can help elderly people by providing companionship.

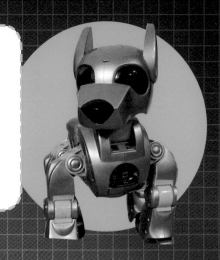

From the heights to the depths

Robotic arms (left) are used to perform tasks in space, as well as under the sea. Robotic arms have been used on the International Space Station to help with building work and repairs. Autonomous underwater vehicles (AUVs) are used to map the ocean bed.

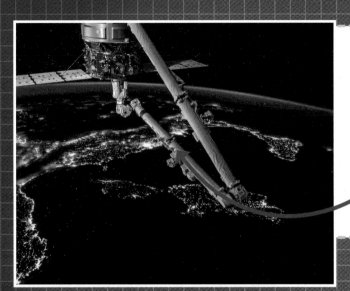

ROBOT ARM IN USE ON THE INTERNATIONAL SPACE STATION

Artificial intelligence

Some robots have artificial intelligence, which means they are able to show some forms of human behaviour. These robots can recognise faces, play games and 'talk'. Some of them even look like people and seem able to make decisions – but that isn't the case. Robots are only tools to help us get things done. Robots are still limited by the information they are given by humans.

Before you get started on each of the projects in this book, you'll need to gather together the materials and tools listed in the 'you will need' box. Hopefully you will have most things to hand but some of the more unusual items can be bought from suppliers listed on page 32.

Basic robot hand

Make a robot hand that moves.

How does it work? When you pull the threads of your robot hand, the drinking straws close up and make the cardboard fingers curl. The drinking straws and threads of the robot hand mimic the action of the bones, tendons, ligaments and muscles in a human hand.

To make a basic robot hand you will need:
- pencil and thin white paper (for tracing the template)
- A4 sheet of thick black paper
- scissors
- tube of clear all-purpose glue
- 5 x drinking straws
- sticky tape
- 5 x lengths of thick thread, 20 cm long

1 Use the template on page 30 to draw and cut out the hand in thick black paper.

2 Make a line of glue down the centre of each of the paper fingers and the thumb.

LINE OF GLUE

3 Cut eleven pieces of drinking straw (three for each of the three middle fingers and two for the little finger). Place them on the lines of glue, leaving a 5 mm gap between each piece.

5 MM GAP

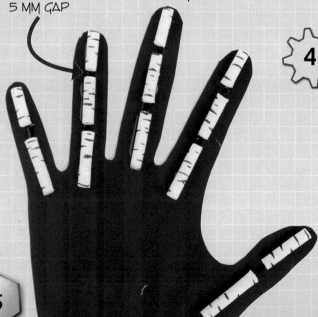

4 Cut two pieces of drinking straw so that they fit on the line of glue on the thumb, leaving a 5 mm gap between each piece. Stick them on the line of glue.

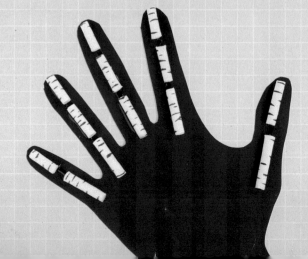

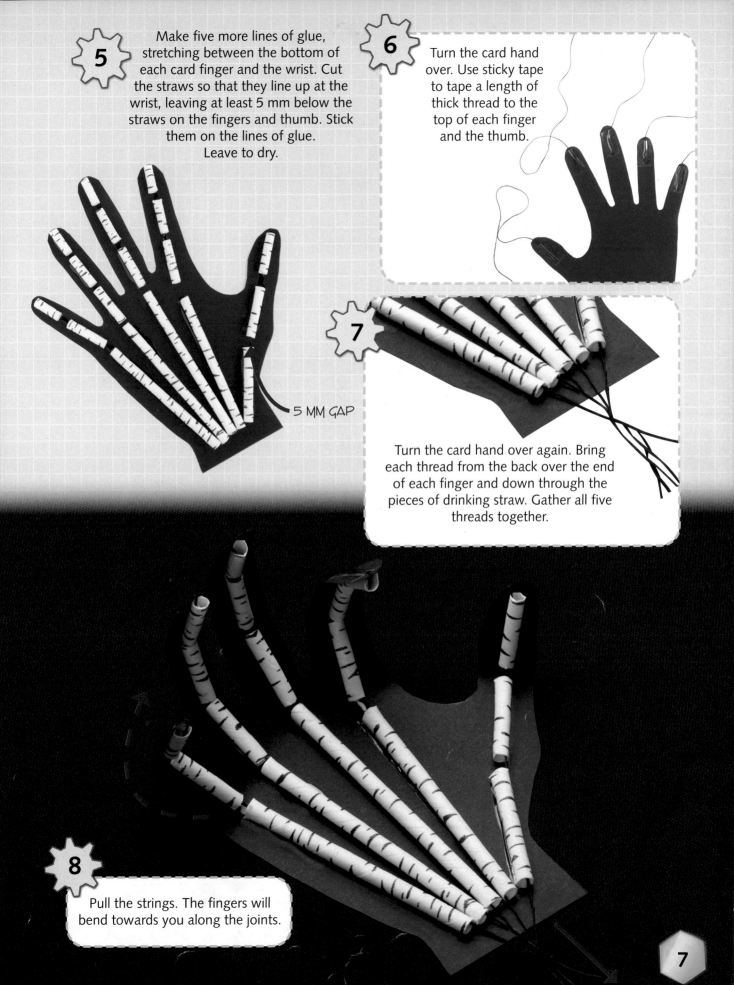

5 Make five more lines of glue, stretching between the bottom of each card finger and the wrist. Cut the straws so that they line up at the wrist, leaving at least 5 mm below the straws on the fingers and thumb. Stick them on the lines of glue. Leave to dry.

5 MM GAP

6 Turn the card hand over. Use sticky tape to tape a length of thick thread to the top of each finger and the thumb.

7 Turn the card hand over again. Bring each thread from the back over the end of each finger and down through the pieces of drinking straw. Gather all five threads together.

8 Pull the strings. The fingers will bend towards you along the joints.

Advanced robotic hand

Amaze your friends with this almost 'human' robotic hand.

The strings in the silicone hand act like the tendons and ligaments in a human hand. The flexible silicone gives the hand weight and substance to carry out simple tasks. Simple prosthetic hands work in a similar way. In real life, users often have to make choices between how well the prosthetic hand works – and how realistic it looks.

To make an advanced robotic hand you will need:

- A4 sheet thin pink craft foam
- pen
- silicone bath sealant gun and tube of sealant
- disposable gloves (available from a DIY store)
- 5 x lengths of string, 50 cm long
- ruler • craft knife
- scissors
- 5 x flexible drinking straws

1 Place your hand on the sheet of craft foam, spreading your fingers wide. Use a pen to draw around your hand.

SAFETY FIRST
This activity should be carried out under adult supervision. Open a window and the door before you use the silicone gun so that you do not breathe in the fumes.

2 Ask an adult to follow the instructions to put the silicone tube into the silicone bath sealant gun and cut off the end of the nozzle. Put on the disposable gloves and draw a line of silicone from the tip of each finger to the wrist on the foam.

3 Take one length of string and carefully lie it along a line of silicone sealant, leaving 15 cm below the wrist. Repeat with the other four pieces of string.

4

Pipe a line of silicone sealant around the hand shape, crossing over each piece of string when you reach it. Fill in the shape with more sealant.

5

Use the craft knife to smooth out the silicone sealant so that it covers the strings. Leave to dry for 24 hours.

Warning!
Silicone sealant takes a long time to dry so do not rush this stage.

6

Cut out the foam hand, taking care not to cut the strings.

7

Turn the hand over so the pink foam faces up.

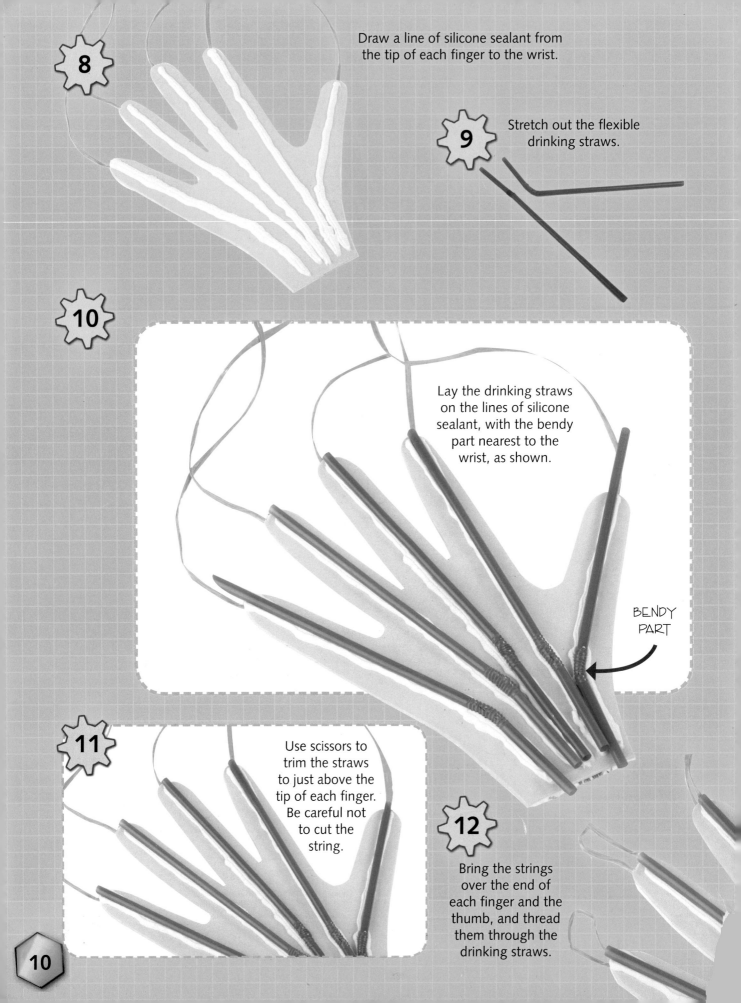

8 Draw a line of silicone sealant from the tip of each finger to the wrist.

9 Stretch out the flexible drinking straws.

10 Lay the drinking straws on the lines of silicone sealant, with the bendy part nearest to the wrist, as shown.

BENDY PART

11 Use scissors to trim the straws to just above the tip of each finger. Be careful not to cut the string.

12 Bring the strings over the end of each finger and the thumb, and thread them through the drinking straws.

13 Cover the hand in silicone sealant, taking care to leave each end of the drinking straws free of silicone.

14 Use the craft knife to smooth out the silicone sealant. Leave until completely dry.

15 Ask an adult to help. Cut small V-shaped notches at the points shown in the photo. Cut through the silicone and the top layer of the drinking straw, but don't cut the string. This will help the fingers to bend.

16

17 Pull the strings to make the silicone hand perform simple tasks, such as gripping a ball.

Glitch Fix!

Glitch: a string was cut by mistake in steps 15/16.

Fix: pull the end back through the straw. Use a knot to reattach it and thread it back through the drinking straw.

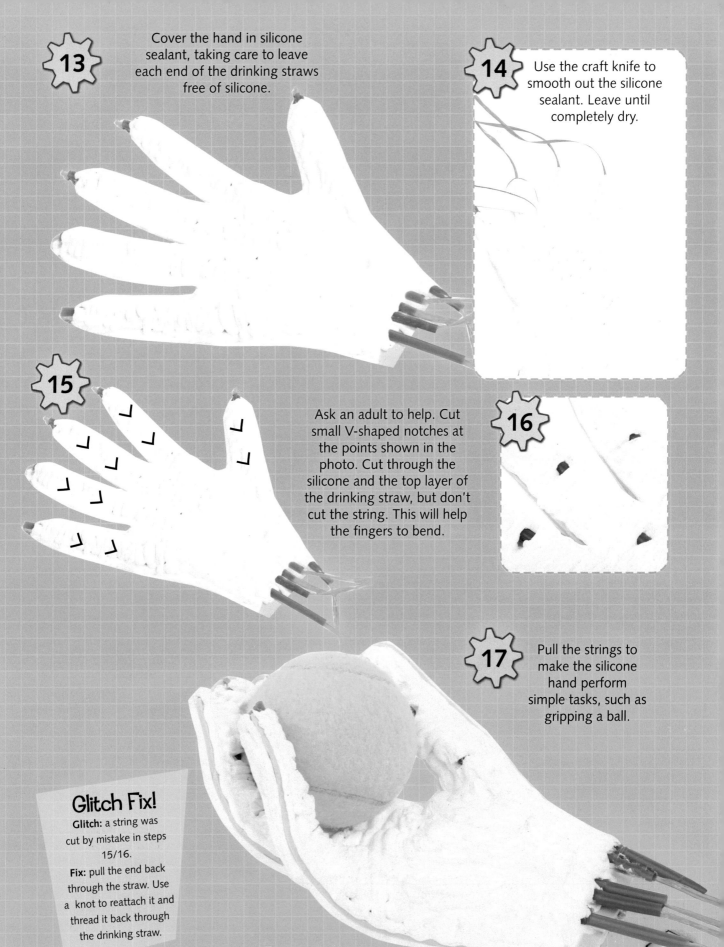

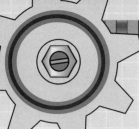

Bristlebot

These fun little robots skitter about at great speed.

How does it move? As the bristlebot's motor vibrates, the vibrations make the bristles on the toothbrush head move and the whole thing 'walks' – moves forward. Bristlebots are small robots made from a toothbrush head and a vibrating motor.

To make a bristlebot you will need:

- battery-powered electric toothbrush (ask permission before you use it for this project)
- pliers
- small scissors
- wire strippers
- double-sided sticky tab (available from craft stores)
- 1.5v button cell battery

1

Carefully use the pliers to snip the head off an electric toothbrush.

Pull off the bottom section of the handle.

2

Use pliers to pull out the insides of the toothbrush. (You will have to pull hard.) Remove the battery – it can be used to power something else.

PULL

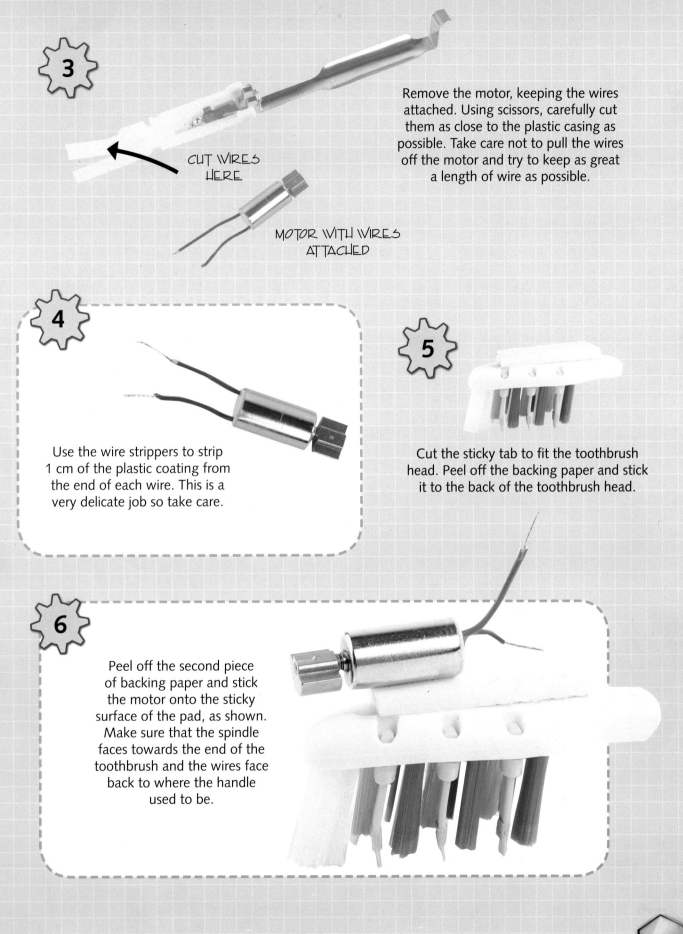

3

CUT WIRES HERE

MOTOR WITH WIRES ATTACHED

Remove the motor, keeping the wires attached. Using scissors, carefully cut them as close to the plastic casing as possible. Take care not to pull the wires off the motor and try to keep as great a length of wire as possible.

4

Use the wire strippers to strip 1 cm of the plastic coating from the end of each wire. This is a very delicate job so take care.

5

Cut the sticky tab to fit the toothbrush head. Peel off the backing paper and stick it to the back of the toothbrush head.

6

Peel off the second piece of backing paper and stick the motor onto the sticky surface of the pad, as shown. Make sure that the spindle faces towards the end of the toothbrush and the wires face back to where the handle used to be.

7 Press the red wire onto the sticky pad and stick a battery on top, with the positive terminal facing down so that the bare red wire comes into contact with that positive terminal. Connect the blue (or black) wire to the top (negative terminal) by bending it onto the battery. Watch your bristlebot go!

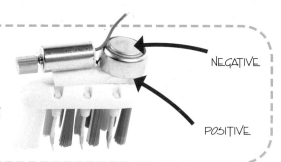

NEGATIVE

POSITIVE

Glitch Fix!

Glitch: bristlebot is not moving very fast.

Fix: place a heavy object on the bristles of the toothbrush head to make the bristles spread out. You'll need to leave it for a few hours.

A fair test

Try racing two bristlebots over a measured distance to see which one goes furthest, fastest and straightest.

To see if you can improve the performance of the winning bristlebot, make a second one that is identical except for one change (see right, for suggestions). Race them again and record the results.

If the change you made does not improve the performance of the bristlebot, or made it worse, change it back and think of another change that might work better. This way you can make your bristlebot into a champion.

Try racing the bristlebots on different surfaces.

POWER SOURCE: YOU COULD SWOP THIS FOR THE MOTOR FROM AN OLD MOBILE PHONE. ASK PERMISSION BEFORE YOU USE IT.

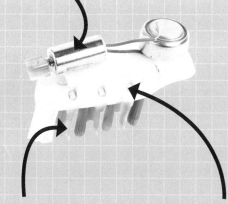

BRISTLES: TRY BENDING THE BRISTLES FURTHER BACK

BODY: TRY USING DIFFERENT TOOTHBRUSH HEADS (THEY DO NOT NEED TO BE FROM AN ELECTRIC TOOTHBRUSH). YOU COULD USE ONE WITH STRAIGHT BRISTLES AND ONE WITH SLANTED BRISTLES

How to design a robot

Teams of designers focus on the coding, the sensors and the mechanical parts of each new robot design.

TACTILE SENSOR

CAMERAS

MOTION TRACKING SENSOR

DISTANCE SENSORS

1. The robot 'brain'

The 'brain' of a robot is run by a computer program using computer codes. The codes give all the instructions the robot needs to function. Robots are being developed with new programming (coding) systems that give the robot the ability to work out the best way of tackling a problem. The simple robots in this book do not have any coding.

To see a video of a product that you could use to program a robot visit:
https://www.youtube.com/watch?v=CqrQmQqpHXc

2. Robot sensors

Robots need to have sensors to tell them about their surroundings. The system of sensors delivers information to the robot brain to allow the robot to do the tasks it was built for. Robots use information about the space between objects, their size and their shape to help them interact with their environment. There are a huge variety of sensors, from ones that detect light, sound and movement, to those that tell the robot the temperature, distance or pressure.

To see a video of robot sensors in action visit:
https://www.youtube.com/watch?v=2STTNYNF4lk

3. Robot body

The 'body' of the robot is the mechanical parts that make it able to grab, turn, lift and move. These are usually powered by air, water, electricity or solar power. In this book you can make robots that grab, move, turn and even draw.

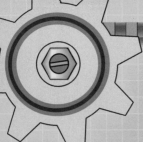

Scrub bot

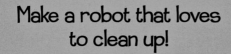

Make a robot that loves to clean up!

How does it do that? The spindle on the small motor that forms part of the scrub bot is weighted to make it vibrate. As the motor vibrates, the vibrations cause the bristles on the nailbrush to vibrate as well, and the scrub bot moves.

To make a scrub bot you will need:

- 1.5v DC motor (available from electronics supplies – see p. 32)
- battery connector
- nailbrush • electrical tape
- slice of wine cork or old eraser, about 5 mm thick
- drawing compass • ruler
- 2 x AA batteries
- AA battery holder
- glue • pipe cleaner
- 2 x googly eyes

1

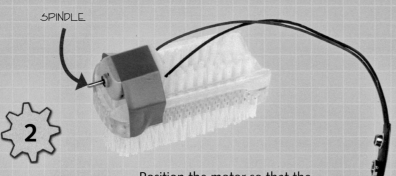

Slide the bare wire sticking out from the red plastic on the battery connector through the metal connector on the motor. Twist it back on itself to keep it in place. Repeat with the other bare wire sticking out from the black plastic-coated wire.

SPINDLE

2

Position the motor so that the spindle is clear of the end of the nailbrush. Tape it in place using electrical tape.

3

Make a small hole 3 mm from the edge of the piece of cork (or eraser) with the point of a compass. Keep this hole as small as possible because it needs to be a tight fit for the motor spindle.

4

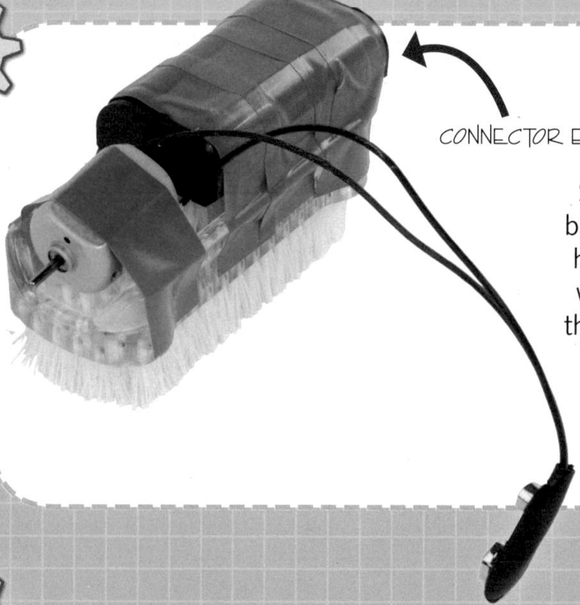

CONNECTOR END

Slot two AA batteries into the battery holder. Place the battery holder on top of the nailbrush, with the connector end facing the opposite way to the spindle. Use electrical tape to fix it in place.

5

Push the cork (or eraser) onto the spindle. If it is loose, take it off and put a small blob of glue into the hole. Replace the cork. Leave to set.

CONNECTORS

6

Curl the ends of the pipe cleaner around, as shown. Glue a googly eye onto each curled up end and glue the eye piece onto the top of the scrub bot.

7

Put your scrub bot on a flat surface and push on the connector. Add some washing-up liquid and water and set your robot to work!

Glitch Fix!

Glitch: the scrub bot is going backwards.
Fix: remove the wires from the motor (step 1) and replace them the other way round.

Drawing robot

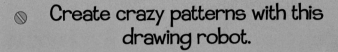

Create crazy patterns with this drawing robot.

How does it work? It uses the vibrations of the motor to make the pens wobble. They draw colourful lines on the paper as the drawing robot moves across the page.

To make a drawing robot you will need:

- disposable cup
- pencil
- square piece of thin card, slightly larger than the top of the cup
- scissors
- drawing compass
- hot glue gun
- 2 x AA batteries
- AA battery holder
- slice of cork, about 5 mm thick
- 1.5v DC motor (available from electronics supplies – see p. 32)
- large paper clip
- 3 x thick felt-tip pens
- masking tape
- large sheet of drawing paper

1 Use a pencil to draw around the top of the disposable cup onto the card. Cut out the card circle.

2 Glue the card circle onto the base of the cup.

SAFETY FIRST
Ask an adult to supervise when you use the hot glue gun.

BATTERY BOX COVER

3 Use the tip of the compass to punch a hole through the centre of the card circle and the base of the cup.

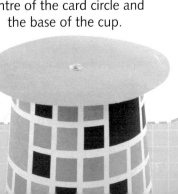

4 Slot two AA batteries into the battery holder. Replace the battery box cover.

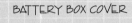

18

SWITCH

5

Use the glue gun to fix the battery box inside the cup. The switch needs to be facing up, close to the opening of the cup.

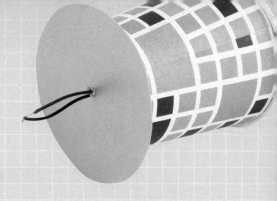

6

Push the black and red electric wires from the battery box through the holes in the base of the cup and the card circle.

7

SPINDLE

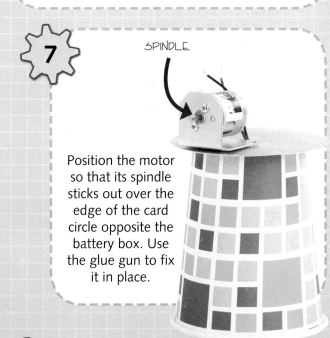

Position the motor so that its spindle sticks out over the edge of the card circle opposite the battery box. Use the glue gun to fix it in place.

8

Attach the red and black wires to the terminals on the motor to complete the electric circuit. Turn the battery pack on briefly to test that the motor is working.

9

Take the slice of cork and use the compass to make a hole, 5 mm from the edge. Push it onto the spindle. It must be a tight fit. If it is loose, take it off and put a small blob of glue into the hole. Replace the cork. Leave to set.

10

Use the glue gun to fix the large paper clip to the front of the cork, as shown. Leave to set.

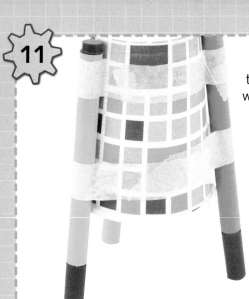

Position the three felt-tip pens around the outside of the cup and secure them with masking tape. Take the lids off. The pen tips now act as feet for the drawing robot.

Place the drawing robot onto a sheet of blank paper. Switch it on and watch the robot draw.

Glitch Fix!

Glitch: if the cup tips over this could be for two reasons. 1) The weight of the battery pack and the motor may not be balanced. **Fix:** see which way the cup is tipping. If it is tipping towards the motor, tape a weight inside the cup opposite the motor. If it is tipping towards the battery pack, tape a weight opposite the battery pack.
2) The pens are not an equal length. Fix: take off the masking tape and move the pens so that the cup is evenly balanced.

Try this!
Use fabric marker pens if you want your robot to make a pattern on a piece of fabric.

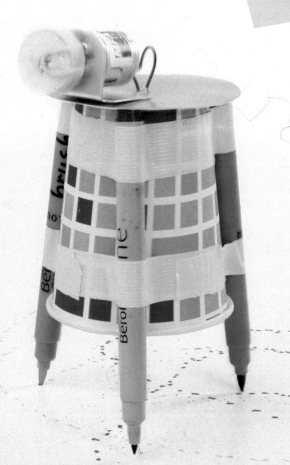

Desktop robot

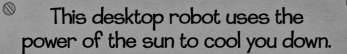

This desktop robot uses the power of the sun to cool you down.

Many service robots perform useful tasks for human beings, such as mowing the lawn, and this one cools you down. Its solar panel, which is coated in a special material, absorbs sunlight and converts it into electrical energy. The energy travels down the wires to drive the motor that is attached to the propeller. The propeller whizzes around creating a cooling flow of air.

To make a desktop robot you will need:

- stiff card, 31 cm x 10 cm
- coloured wrapping paper, 31 cm x 10 cm
- ruler
- pencil
- glue and spreader
- craft knife
- micro motor (4v solar micro motor 47000rpm), propeller and solar panel kit (available from electronics suppliers – see p. 32)
- small screwdriver

1 Cover one side of the card with glue. Stick on the coloured wrapping paper. Leave to dry.

2 Turn the card over. Use the ruler and pencil to make marks 10 cm apart. Fold the card along the edge of the ruler at each 10 cm mark and along the 1 cm tab mark at the end.

1 CM   10 CM   10 CM   10 CM

3 Use the ruler and pencil to draw diagonal lines across each 10 cm square section of card.

4 Place the motor where the lines cross on the end section. Draw around the motor. Ask an adult to help you cut out the card circle using a craft knife.

5 Make a small hole in the centre of the middle section of the card using the point of the screwdriver.

6 Turn the card over. Push the motor into place in the hole you made in step 4. Make sure the spindle faces out on the patterned side and add the propeller.

7 Push the wires connected to the solar panel through the small hole in the middle section of the card.

8 Glue the solar panel in place in the centre of the middle panel.

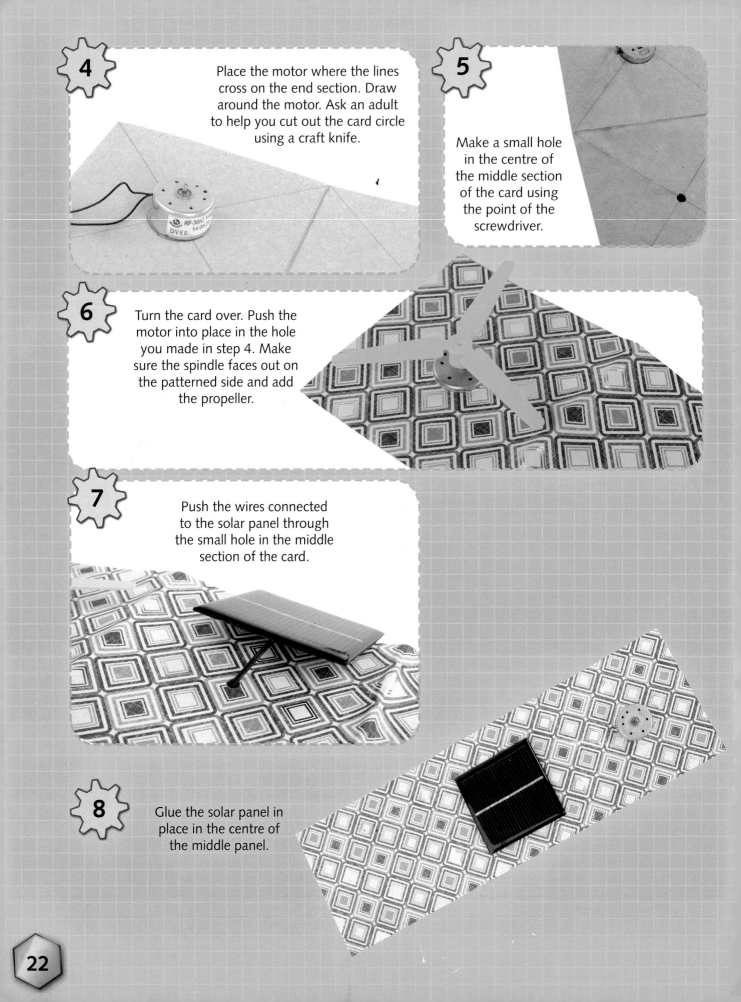

9

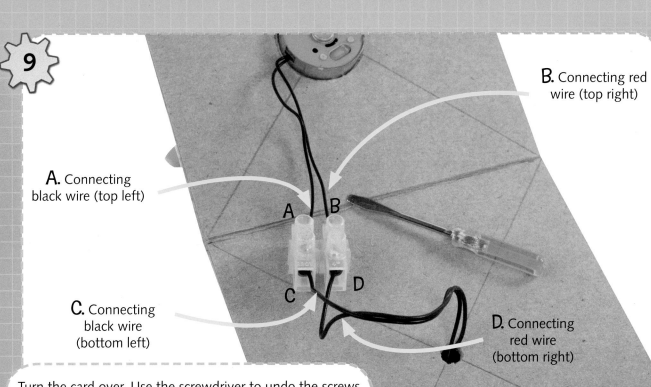

A. Connecting black wire (top left)

B. Connecting red wire (top right)

C. Connecting black wire (bottom left)

D. Connecting red wire (bottom right)

Turn the card over. Use the screwdriver to undo the screws in the plastic connection box a little, leaving a small space under the tip of each screw.

A. Slide the metal end of a black wire under the tip of the screw marked A. Tighten the screw to hold it in place.

B. Slide the metal end of a red wire under the tip of the screw marked B. Tighten the screw to hold it in place.

C. Slide the metal end of a black wire under the tip of the screw marked C. Tighten the screw to hold it in place.

D. Slide the metal end of a red wire under the tip of the screw marked D. Tighten the screw to hold it in place.

10 Spread glue on the card side of the 1 cm flap. With the propeller and the solar panel on the outside, stick the flap to the card side of the end section to form a triangular prism.

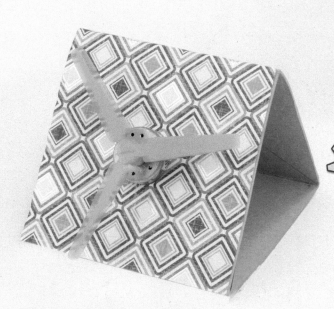

11 Place the desktop robot on a desk where strong sunlight or a bright desk lamp will fall on the solar panel. The solar panel will use the light to generate electrical energy, which will pass down the wires and make the motor spin the propeller around.

Robbo the robot

Build your own Robbo the robot!

You can use a gear box and an electric motor powered by batteries to make a robot that runs on wheels and moves its arms. To do this, you attach a gear box kit to a metal axle, with wheels attached. When you turn the motor on, it turns the back axle of Robbo, making it move forwards and moving its arms at the same time.

To make Robbo the robot you will need:

- craft knife
- ruler
- crisp tube with lid
- marker pen
- Phillips screwdriver
- pen • measuring tape • scissors
- silver spray paint • patterned strong paper drinking straw
- 3v worm drive gear box kit (available from electronics suppliers – see p. 32)
- hot glue gun
- 2 x elastic bands
- 2 x wooden skewers, 12 cm long
- 4 x plastic caps (from small plastic drink bottles)
- nail and hammer • offcut of wood
- wooden craft stick (available from craft stores)
- 2 x polystyrene balls, 8 cm and 1.5 cm diameter

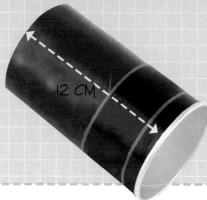

12 CM

1 Use the ruler and pen to mark a line around the crisp tube, 12 cm from the top. Ask an adult to cut off this section using a craft knife.

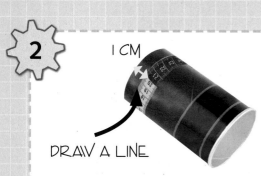

1 CM

DRAW A LINE

2 Wrap the measuring tape around the cut edge of the tube, 1 cm from the edge. Draw a line above the edge of the measuring tape.

7 CM

3 Make two marks 7 cm apart along the line. Use the screwdriver to make a hole at each mark.

4 Enlarge the holes by pushing the end of a pen into them and twisting it. They need to be just large enough for a drinking straw to slide through.

5 Cut two slots on the other side of the tube, 8 cm apart and 4.5 cm from the holes made in step 3 (see diagram in step 7).

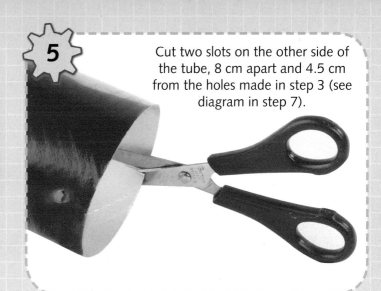

6 Make a hole at the top of each slit with the screwdriver. They need to be large enough for the axles attached to the gear box to rotate freely (see p. 26).

7 The tube should look like this from the top.

8 CM

SLOT WITH HOLE AT THE TOP FOR AXLE (SEE STEP 6)

TUBE FROM TOP

SLOT WITH HOLE AT THE TOP FOR AXLE (SEE STEP 6)

4.5 CM

4.5 CM

HOLE FOR STRAW (SEE STEP 3)

7 CM

HOLE FOR STRAW (SEE STEP 3)

8

Spray the tube with silver paint. Leave to dry.

Warning!
Open the window and the door before you use the spray paint so that you do not breathe in the fumes.

25

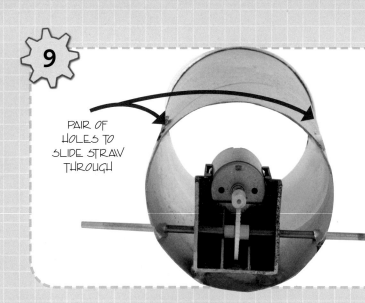

PAIR OF HOLES TO SLIDE STRAW THROUGH

Slide the axle into the two slots and into the holes you made in steps 5–6. Use the glue gun to glue the plastic part of the motor inside the tube. Leave to dry.

Slide a paper drinking straw through the top pair of holes you made in steps 3–4.

SAFETY FIRST
Ask an adult to supervise when you use the hot glue gun.

10

Turn the model around. Attach the wires from the battery pack to the motor. Glue the battery pack to the inside of the tube, with the switch near to the uncut edge of the tube.

11

Slide one side of the axle out of the slot. Slide an elastic band over the end of the axle. Push the axle back through the slot so that the elastic band is between the motor and the slot. Repeat with the other side of the axle.

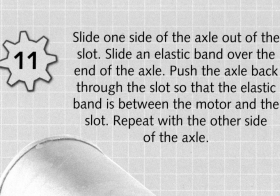

SLOT

12

Use the ruler to make a mark, 4 cm from the top edge and in between the axle and the drinking straw. Use the screwdriver to make a hole at this point and repeat on the opposite side of the tube.

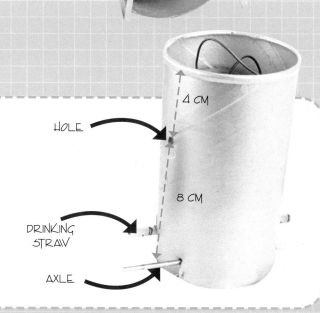

4 CM

HOLE

8 CM

DRINKING STRAW

AXLE

13 Feed the elastic bands up to the top of the tube, near what will become the arm holes. Slide a wooden skewer through the hole in the tube you created in step 12, through both the elastic bands and through the hole opposite.

14 Place a bottle cap on the offcut of wood. Hold the nail so that the point is exactly in the centre of the cap. Tap the nail gently with the hammer to make a hole. Remove the nail. Repeat with the other three bottle caps.

15 Spray the bottle caps with silver paint. Leave to dry.

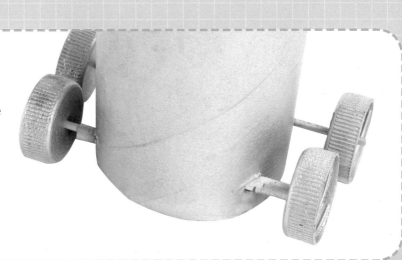

16 Slide a wooden skewer through the drinking straw. Push a bottle cap onto each end to give Robbo wheels. Leave about 5 mm of skewer sticking out. Repeat to add wheels to the other axle.

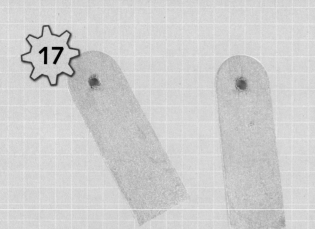

17

Use scissors to cut the wooden craft stick in half. Make a small hole in the middle of one end with a screwdriver, 1 cm from the top edge. Repeat with the other half. Spray the craft sticks silver. Leave to dry.

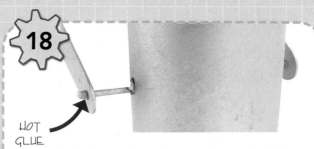

18

HOT GLUE

Push the craft sticks onto the ends of the wooden skewer you attached in step 13 in order to make arms for Robbo. If the skewer is not a tight fit, glue it in place with the hot glue gun.

19

Ask an adult to cut the large polystyrene ball in half. Use the glue gun to stick one half onto the lid of the crisp tube.

Glue the small polystyrene ball onto the large polystyrene ball. Spray the whole thing with silver paint. Leave to dry.

Glitch Fix!

Glitch: the arms do not move.
Fix: the elastic band is too loose or too tight. Try different sizes of elastic band until you find one that works.

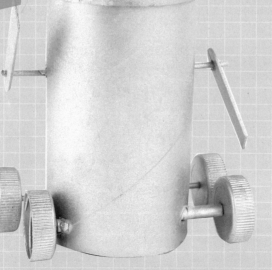

20

Switch on the motor. Push the lid in place to give Robbo a head. Place Robbo on a flat surface and off he whizzes!

Try this!

Decorate Robbo with paint or stickers. Add details such as hair, hands and eyes.

Milestones in the history of robots

Greek philosopher and mathematician, Archytas of Tarentum, built a wooden bird that could flap its wings.

400 BCE

1495

Leonardo da Vinci drew plans for a humanoid robot that could move its head and sit up.

1700-1900

Automatons, mechanical puppets of animals or figures, became popular. The most famous of them was a mechanical duck, designed by Jacques de Vaucanson, which could stretch its neck, flap its wings and swallow and digest food.

British mathematician, Charles Babbage, started work on his Analytical Machine, one of the first computational machines.

1833

The word 'robot' was first used in a play by Czech writer Karel Capek. In the play, an inventor creates human-like machines, called robots, and the people in the play are killed or enslaved by them.

1921

1932

The first robot toy, called the Lilliput, was produced in Japan. It was a tin wind-up toy that could walk.

American writer Isaac Asimov introduced the three laws of robotics in his story, *Runaround*.

1942

1943

1950

British mathematician, Alan Turing, devised a test to see if a computer can really think for itself. This test has become known as the 'Turing Test'.

The world's first electronic computer, Colossus, was built in Britain to crack Nazi coded messages.

The Stanford Cart was one of the first mobile robots controlled by computers. It was able to navigate across a room full of chairs.

1961

The first industrial robot was used on the assembly line at General Motors in the USA to make cars.

American engineer, Victor Scheinman, developed a programmable robot arm, which became widely used in factories.

1975

1981

Canadarm, a remotely operated 'arm', performed its first tasks in space.

NASA's Sojourner robot rover carried out a series of science experiments on Mars.

1997

2000

The United Nations estimated that there were 742,500 industrial robots in use worldwide.

The tiny da Vinci robot was first used in heart surgery in Canada to unblock a patient's arteries.

2007

2002

The Roomba robotic vacuum cleaner was sold in large numbers.

Robots are an important part of our everyday lives.

Today

29

Template

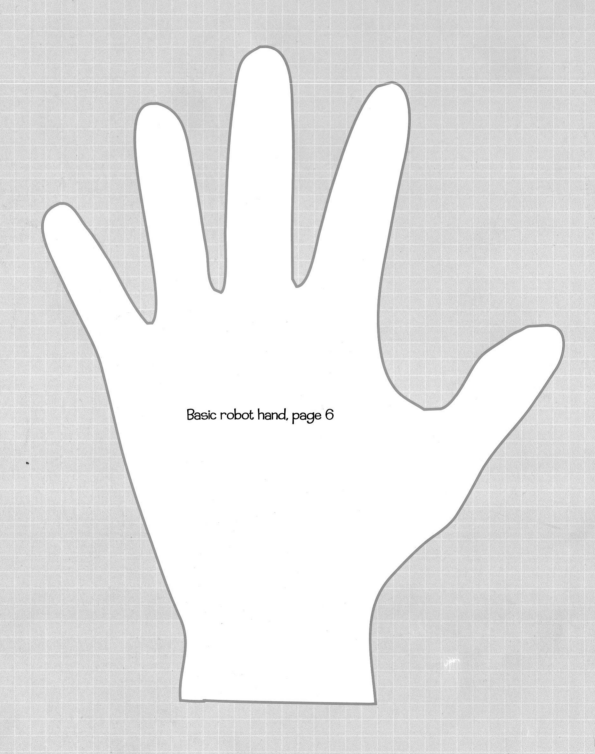

Basic robot hand, page 6

Glossary

Artificial intelligence An area of computer science dedicated to making computers copy intelligent human behaviour.

Autonomous underwater vehicle A programmable underwater robotic vehicle.

Blood vessels Tubes (veins, arteries and capillaries) that carry blood around the body.

Contaminated An object or area that has been poisoned or made hazardous in some way.

Ligament A short band of tough, fibrous material that connects two bones together.

Mechanical The working parts of a machine.

Prosthesis An artificial limb.

Radiation A type of dangerous energy that is produced by radioactive substances.

Sensor A device that detects or measures things.

Service robot A robot that performs useful tasks for humans.

Spindle The rotating small metal rod attached to an electric motor.

Tendon A tough flexible cord of fibrous material that attaches a muscle to a bone.

Vibration A quick forward and back movement.

Further information

Make your own Mars rover:
http://www.nasa.gov/sites/default/files/atoms/files/mars_survival_
kit_-_rover_final_4.pdf

Drive a Mars rover without draining all of its battery power:
http://www.nasa.gov/audience/foreducators/robotics/home/ROVER.
html#.VmbUA7TJt0I

Help *Crash* build a robot to help with his chores:
http://www.wonderville.ca/asset/robot-factory

Watch a video of a really cool robot:
http://www.wimp.com/coolestrobot/

Explore the Lego Mindstorms website to find out more about its create
and command Lego robot sets:
http://www.lego.com/en-gb/mindstorms

Note to parents and teachers: every effort has been made by the
Publishers to ensure that these websites are suitable for children,
that they are of the highest educational value, and that they
contain no inappropriate or offensive material. However, because
of the nature of the Internet, it is impossible to guarantee that
the contents of these sites will not be altered.
We strongly advise that Internet access is supervised by
a responsible adult.

Index

Crafts and parts suppliers

Craft shops, art shops, office suppliers and stationery shops will sell
most of the materials you will need to build the models in this book –
and you will be able to use materials you have at home or at school.

A good online craft store is: www.bakerross.co.uk

This electronics supplier sells electric motors and other related
components:
www.maplin.co.uk
To buy silicone bath sealant and a dispensing gun, visit any DIY store,
or ask an adult to order from: www.fredaldous.co.uk